Physician, Heal Thyself

William F. Johnson

Table of Contents

Other Books by William F Johnson

- Leading Your Ministry to Financial Health
  http://www.aslanpress.com/financial-leadership.html
- Motivation: Your Guide to Fitting In
  http://www.aslanpress.com/motivation.html
- Destiny: Who Am I? Why Am I Here, What Do I Do Now?
  http://www.aslanpress.com/destiny.html
- Physician, Heal Thyself: The Oxygen Mask Principle
  http://www.aslanpress.com/physician-heal-thyself.html

- Pray Like Jesus
  http://aslanpress.com/pray-like-jesus.html
- Built To Last
  http://www.aslanpress.com/built-to-last.html

Dedication.

This book is dedicated to the givers in this world, pastors, doctors, nurses and others who spend themselves serving others.

Acknowledgements.

I would also like to acknowledge my wife, Rita, for her contribution of material and research for this project; Beth Wynn for her love, support and editing skills; Ron and Rebecca Bounds, Larry and Natalie Dautenhahn, and Bruce and Elaine Wimberley for their love and support of us and Aslan Ministries. We would also like to acknowledge the leadership and encouragement of Reverend Dave and Jan Walker who first introduced us to the ministry of healing thirty years ago.

Introduction

Each day, it seems we have new charges brought against celebrities for sexual abuse. The church is not immune from these crimes. In fact we regularly read of Priests, Pastors, and ministry leaders that fall into sexual and abusive sin. Several years ago, my wife and I began to hear of these atrocities and decided to do something. We researched why and how this happens, interviewed victims and perpetrators, then put together and taught several workshops for pastors and leaders to help them avoid falling.

Those who give of themselves - to others - are vulnerable to burn out, depression, and compassion fatigue. This can lead to physical and emotional illness, addiction, dependence, and a loss of one's moral compass.

Surveys have shown that:

- Fifteen hundred pastors leave the ministry each month due to moral failure, spiritual burnout, or contention in their churches.
- Fifty percent of pastors' marriages will end in divorce.

- Ninety percent of pastors report working between fifty five and seventy five hours per week

- Eighty percent believe pastoral ministry has negatively affected their families.

Is it any wonder that these professions have such a high dropout rate? Why are these givers subject to moral failure? How can we change this problem? That is the question this book tries to answer.

This book is written to provide guidance and healing to those who are giving of themselves to others. Our goal for the reader is a fruitful and lasting life of serving God and His people.

William (Bill) F. Johnson,
President, Aslan Ministries, Inc.

1. The Oxygen Mask Principle

Luke 4:23(KJV) And he said unto them, Ye will surely say unto me this proverb, Physician, heal thyself:

On every airline flight throughout the world flight attendants welcome the passengers aboard with a flurry of announcements. The most important is the safety announcement that most ignore. No matter how creative the attendant is with the life jacket and oxygen mask demonstrations, they are barely noticed. But, if you listen very carefully you will discover the single most important principle which may save your ministry and your life. The demonstration of proper oxygen mask attachment ends with this instruction,

> *"If you are traveling with someone who needs your assistance, put your mask on first before you help them."*

That statement should be placed on the mirror of all care givers: pastors, nurses, doctors, parents and everyone who is responsible for the physical or spiritual care of others. You will not be able to help others if you are dying or impaired by oxygen depletion.

We can safely say that there are many ministers throughout the world who ignore this principle to the detriment of themselves and also the people they are called to serve. This is a major reason why ministers of all types find their calling so difficult. My first few years in ministry were overwhelming. There were so many needs that I attempted to meet that I became burned out and discouraged.

Ministry is extremely challenging. There are two directions from which challenges originate; (1) our own personal issues and (2) challenges imposed upon us from the outside.

Internal factors

Theologian and author Don Williams writes,

"Most churches are dysfunctional and most pastors are co-dependent."[1]

There are many doctors, nurses, and pastors who enter ministry because of their own needs, rather than an altruistic desire to help others. They may have a great need to be loved; they believe that people will love them if they minister to their needs. They think to themselves, "If I take care of people, they will love me. I will be loved and accepted." Ministers with this deep need to be loved are very susceptible to burn out. They are driven to give, but do not put boundaries on their giving.

Another factor is the attraction to ministry of people who have a strong desire for control. While often spiritually deadly to both the pastor and church, there seems to be a great number of control freaks in ministering medically and spiritually today. This is often the result of an Obsessive-Compulsive Disorder (OCD). An obsession is a particular thought repeated over and over again to the point that it is difficult to dislodge from the mind. Such obsessions usually result in frequent behavior patterns known as compulsions. In its extreme, obsessive compulsive behavior takes the form of agoraphobia, panic attacks, an inability to sleep, and sometimes even difficulty in functioning at all. Cable television viewers were treated to the ultimate OCD in the character of Adrian Monk played so well by Tony Shalhoub. Needless to say most OCD's don't get that far out, but many of us will pat our pocket to see if the wallet is still there or are married to the wife who calls three times to remind us to stop at the store.

Not all OCD behavior is negative. Frank Minerth[2], who admits to being an OCD, has developed a list of one hundred twenty nine characteristics of an OCD. Number one twenty eight reads, "They like to make lists." I relate well to a few of the items on Minerth's list.

- Arrives within 60 seconds of an appointment.
- In Psychological stress test he will be in the top 5 %
- "I'll do it myself"
- Become detail oriented.
- Project directed,

The Bible contains many OCD's. Mary and Martha were friends and followers of Jesus. Martha, (the OCD)[3], considered the project of having the Savior for dinner more important than acknowledging the Person of Jesus Christ. She labored far too hard over the project and criticized her sister Mary who was sitting at Jesus' feet. Martha felt motivated to control Mary as well as Jesus. Moses, another OCD, experienced a miracle[4] as God produced water from a rock. Later God told Moses to speak to the rock to receive the water.[5] But Moses decided he would strike the rock with his staff as he had done previously. This is a prime example of an OCD in action. The water did come forth, but because of Moses' unbelief and his stubborn OCD tendencies; he was not allowed access to the Promised Land. Many pastors and church leaders are susceptible to OCD behavior. They believe they can achieve complete control over their life and the church if they only work hard enough.

> *Isaiah 40:31 (KJV)* [31] *But they that wait upon the LORD shall renew their strength; they shall mount up with wings as eagles; they shall run, and not be weary; and they shall walk, and not faint.*

Ministers of the gospel are human but believe that they should live a holy life. Unfortunately they are subject to the same temptations as the people they serve; [6] the lust of the flesh (sexual and physical enticements), lust of the eyes (materialism), and pride of life (power struggles). OCD's may fall into sexual temptation more often than others because of their tendency to deny emotions and their own sexuality. When their need for emotional intimacy is not fulfilled within the home, they may look for that intimacy in inappropriate places. OCD's may also tend to be tempted materialistically and may find themselves involved in power struggles.

Another internal factor that affects ministers is that some of the very people to which they are ministering will be hurtful. Hurting people hurt people. The old adage,"Sheep bite," is very true. Ministers, by definition, provide care for individuals who often do not receive that care graciously. Anyone who has been in ministry for more than a few years knows what it feels like to be hurt by someone you are trying to help.

A hurting minister will begin to set up defensive walls. Over a period of time this may result in what John Sandford[7] refers to as a "Heart of Stone."[8] There are two kinds of hearts of stone. The first kind is very obvious; it is the hard hearted person who does not care about anyone or anything except themselves. We say, "His heart is so hard he will never help."

Secular counselors and medical personnel are taught to not become personally involved in their client or patient's issues, but those in Christian ministry normally care deeply for the people we serve. (It is one reason why they are often more successful.) As a result, Christian ministers cannot always maintain an objective attitude.

The second kind of heart of stone is less obvious. It is the hidden heart of stone. People with the hidden heart of stone will act loving, will minister to others, and will always be ready to help others. But they will never let anyone minister to them. They are extremely loving and outgoing but will never let anyone know what is in their own heart. Those with this hidden heart of stone fear real intimacy. They will not let anyone get close enough to hurt them. When a relationship begins to grow intimate, they will deliberately do something mean to drive the other person away. Those with the hidden heart of stone are prone to fall into sexual sin because they are often covering up feelings that they are afraid to express.

It was many years into our marriage when I learned about my hidden heart of stone. It was while listening to John Sandford.[9] On our honeymoon in Jamaica, I had become angry at my wife Rita for some of the most trivial items - most notably, the way she drove the golf cart. When I understood this hidden heart of stone, I realized that we were becoming too close, and I was fearful of this intimacy. My defensive walls had been developed over many years and her love for me was breaking through. I felt threatened; my anger pushed her away, and my walls were again safe. At the time something like this occurs, we may not know the true root of the problem, but once the root is exposed healing can be realized.

While these internal factors will affect how a person ministers, they are not all bad. They must be understood so that they will not be harmful to the minister or the people receiving ministry.

EXTERNAL FACTORS

There are also external factors which rob ministers of their joy in ministry. First, there is so much demand upon anyone in ministry. The number of people in one's family, church, city, and area who need ministry can be overwhelming. As that expands to your, region, nation, and to the world the numbers are multiplied. Jesus said,

> *"You will be my witnesses in Jerusalem, and in all Judea and Samaria, and to the ends of the earth."*[10]

If someone is at all conscientious about this call, he carries a heavy load. In years past, one pastor could minister to a church of two to three hundred or more parishioners using a dedicated group of lay volunteers. Today it is common for both husband and wife to have careers and many outside interests. As a result, the church volunteer list has decreased and there is less involvement in the ministry of the church by the laity. Statistics now show that it takes one paid staff person for every sixty to seventy parishioners to meet the demands of the church. In the past that number was as high as two hundred parishioners to one paid staff person. As a result pastors work harder for longer hours and still find themselves falling behind. There is so much to do, so few workers, and so little time.

Another external issue which faces ministers contentious patients or parishioners. If a minister wants to make changes, he must realize that wherever there is movement there will also be friction. Friction plus movement equals heat. A Boy Scout with two sticks can create a bonfire. A disgruntled member with two allies can create a lot of heat for the minister.

Then there are those people who will never be satisfied. They may have been wounded by a previous minister or a previous church and they are still angry and bitter. They will spill out their hurt on the current minister who wonders where he went wrong. While it may seem to be personal with the current minister, it is not. They were hurt by a former pastor or church member. They are only taking their hurt or frustration out on the current leader. Ministers cannot take these actions personally. Chapter 4 will deal with conflict resolution.

2. Burn Out

Mark 6:31 (KJV) [31] *And he said unto them, Come ye yourselves apart into a desert place, and rest a while: for there were many coming and going, and they had no leisure so much as to eat.*

Burn out is a common term, but it may manifest itself in three different kinds of damage: burn out, wounding, and depression[11].

Burn out happens only to givers. Its nature is the depletion of the giver's physical and emotional resources. Adam Grant[12] explains that there are three types of people, "Givers," "Takers," and "Matchers." Givers always give more than they get from others. Takers are those who always get more than they give, while matchers always want to keep balance. Matchers keep score to ensure that they keep scales balanced. They want something in return for what they give.

Grant explains,

"By and large, because of their tendencies toward powerful speech and claiming credit, successful takers tend to dominate the spotlight. But if you start

paying attention to reciprocity styles in your own workplace, I have a hunch that you'll discover plenty of givers achieving the success to which you aspire."

Grant identifies two kinds of givers. There is the "selfless" giver who is often taken advantage of by others. He is a super candidate for early burn out. He will also have a difficult time completing his own work and as a result may often be passed over for promotion. As I began to follow Jesus, it was difficult for me to say no to someone who had a need or when there was an assignment in the church. For Rita it was a similar thing. We are both were Type A personalities and wanted to be helpful. Soon we both began to run dry and burn out. We had become "selfless" givers. It was Rita who first learned to say, "No!" It took me a lot longer.

Grant refers to the second type of giver as the "otherish" giver. The otherish giver thrives while helping others to achieve their goals while still working effectively. Grant demonstrates that the "otherish" giver will be more successful in an organization than the "takers" or "matchers" who have similar positions. The "selfless" givers give without regard to their own needs and tend to be overlooked and will burn out early. The "otherish" givers consider their own time and efforts important, but are always willing to help others.

	Concern for others interests →	
Selfish Takers	**Otherish Successful Givers**
Apathetic	**Selfless Self-Sacrificing Givers**

(Concern for self Interest — vertical axis)

Before a commercial airliner takes off, we hear the cabin attendant make the obligatory gas mask announcement. They always conclude with a statement appropriate to givers, "If you are assisting someone else with their gasmask, put your mask on first, and then assist your fellow passenger." That has to be the approach you use in your generosity.

Burnout has become a useful term in the last decade or two. Its use is reflective of a heightened awareness of a widespread problem among those who expend themselves in service to others. In my opinion, this condition actually involves three kinds of damage, of which burn out is only one. Depression and wounding are the other two.[13]

Burn outs are those who are the selfless givers. They have too little consciousness of their personal needs to do what is necessary to replenish themselves from the intensity of giving. Time and rest will usually cure burn out; the same cannot be said for depression and wounding.

Depression is often the result of one's performance orientation. Performance orientation arises from the belief that we are what we do. Our self worth comes from what we can do rather than who we are. We believe that we are loved only when we perform and we are not loved when we do not perform. For the performance oriented person, the hope of love and the ability to accept one's self always centers about the meeting of expectations. Deep depression comes about which can only be resolved by self acceptance and the realization that God's love s free. We cannot earn God's love nor can we lose God's love.[14]

Wounding is an emotional condition caused by the hurtful acts of others. Anyone can experience wounding, but it is especially severe for those who are givers by nature or by profession. We cannot fall back on professional detachment. If a person is going to be healed there must be a close bond between healer and the one to be healed. When you have poured out yourself in the interest of another, when you have given all of yourself to another you become vulnerable to pain and wounding as that person turns on you.

Jesus said our life would have trial and tribulations.[15] Life will serve up many hurts, betrayals and abandonments which take time to heal, but when they come too quickly or hurt too deeply we are not able to recover effectively.

We often forget the humanity of Jesus. Jesus rested because He was tired. In John chapter four, we see Jesus leaving Jerusalem and going to Galilee with his followers. There had been problems in Jerusalem with the religious leaders so the left and headed to Galilee. They took the road down from Jerusalem to Jericho, and then left the Jordan Valley up to Sychar where Jacob's well was located. Jesus was tired and sat down by the well while his disciples went into the town to get something to eat. We often think that our Christian work ethic would have us push on to Galilee, but Jesus listened to His body and rested. As a result, a whole Samarian town of Sychar became believers. Many of us "Type A" personalities mistakenly believe the only good Christian is a busy one!

Sandford[16] proposes three stages of wounding. We can just as easily consider these as appropriate for burn out or depression.

Stage I

Conventional wisdom focuses on preventing burn out, but this may not always be the best approach. Sometimes burn out becomes a tool for the Lord to help the servant realize the need for God's strength in ministry. In Stage I we are still running under our own strength and so we begin to suffer adrenal burn out. Adrenal burn out occurs when the adrenal gland has over produced for such a long time that it no longer functions properly. We then become addicted to stress. We actually subconsciously need and create stressful situations so that the fear, the pressure, and the resulting adrenaline production overcomes our fatigue. For example, given a light load, I usually produce mediocre work, but given an overload situation I work at peak form and often deliver excellent results.

On a trip to Russia in the early 1990's I was scheduled to teach a class at their equivalent of the National Bureau of

Standards. This was at the time that the Soviet Bloc was beginning to fall apart and our trip became questionable. The trip was on again, off again, so we were not able to plan very far ahead. When the final decision was made there were less than two weeks to prepare. In thirteen days we put together a twenty four hour presentation with graphics and over two thousand pages of student handouts. We left Seattle in early evening flying to Copenhagen where, after a couple of hours layover, we boarded a plane to Moscow with a stop in Stockholm. We arrived in Moscow in late afternoon local time and checked into our hotel and crashed. Each day was a new adventure. My energy level was out of sight: working, teaching, and enjoying the city. It was exhilarating. We lived on adrenalin and Russian food with little sleep. It was not unlike our existence back home; taking seminary classes, with the pressure of writing, studying, and exams; working full time and helping to plant a church.

As I look back over my life, I see a common thread of a high level of achievement only when there was a difficult challenge. Many times I would create a crisis situation by waiting until the last minute to accomplish a task. Whenever I started a task early, I quickly became bored and would goof off for awhile (waiting for inspiration?) Maybe you have done something similar. Then at the last minute, I would pour on the coal, work all night, and often the product was better than if I had plodded through.

Before I met Jesus Christ, I considered myself a "workaholic". When I became a Christian, I became a reformed workaholic. What does this mean? It means that then I could leave the office and forget about my job. But then go home change clothes, gulp down a quick meal and run off to the church for a committee meeting, a Bible study or to meet someone who needed my help. Sure, I was no longer a workaholic at the office, but my need for pressure and stress which stimulated me to work at peak performance came from doing things at church. Who could argue with that? Everything I was doing was for Jesus. My wife Rita was first to say it. "Slow down, we are too busy." But I insisted that I could handle all that I was doing and more besides. If someone would ask me to do something more, I would just hitch up my pants, and take on another job. After awhile I would learn about overload.

It is not easy to minister to someone who is in stage one burn out. They are still having too much fun and the adrenalin rush keeps them going.

Stage II

At stage II, burn out or wounding, stress addiction begins to fail as a motivator. Stage II victims begin to find it difficult to remember life without exhaustion. They cannot remember when they were not tired. The digestive system reacts to the stress by producing more acid and other chemicals than the system is designed to handle, often resulting in ulcers, colitis, food allergies, and diarrhea. Colds, aches, pains, sore throats, and headaches increase in frequency and intensity. Whenever I went on the road to teach a class or was faced with a difficult situation, my sinuses would swell up, I would get a sore throat and my voice would become hoarse and raspy.

At this stage we begin to feel as if we are ministering with an empty bucket that is not being refilled. Desperation sets in and we go to the well, but nothing is there. We become functionally blind to the effectiveness of our ministry. We become angry with those who take up our time. We begin to withdraw even from those who offer love. We treat them as if they were demanding more of our time.

In stage two we begin to become angry with God. In our eyes, God has not been a protector. He may be there for others, through us, but seldom for us. We feel as though God has let us down. It is then that our prayer life suffers. We can still hope, but it is common to have periods of despair, and sudden impulses to weep over silly things. After a difficult trip to the East coast I was returning home to the Pacific Northwest. As the Boeing 757 backed out from the gate, the flight attendant began the announcements.

"Welcome aboard our flight today to beautiful Seattle, my hometown." Suddenly I just started weeping and could not understand why. I was in stage two burn out.

Ministry to Stage II

Mark 6:31 "Come with me to a quiet place and get some rest. "

If approached at the right time and under the right circumstances, someone in Stage II can still spill his hurt and receive ministry. He doesn't usually want a solution or unasked for advice. He just needs a safe place to dump. It may help to kidnap him and take him out for a fun time. Richard, my golfing buddy would knock on the door. When

Rita opened the door, he would ask, "Can Bill come out to play?"

It is always good to intercede for someone in prayer, but when a person is in Stage Two, it should be done from a distance. If the Lord gives you a specific scripture or prophecy for him, give it to him in writing. It will feed his hope. Don't confront him face to face with it, but leave it so he can read it and respond in private.

Stage III

People who are in Stage III, burn out or wounding, are so deeply wounded that they can only be carried, not exhorted. They need to be loved, not instructed. Many in the body of Christ expect a quick fix. They seek and expect instantaneous miracles.

They will think or say, "If he had enough faith, he wouldn't be in this fix." or "Give it up to the Lord," or "What he needs is deliverance from demonic spirits."

There are no such miracles for a third stage and he knows it. He is frightened by simplistic solutions to his desperate problem.

He feels physically sick all the time. The constant flow

of adrenalin erodes the connective tissues resulting in aches and pains in joints and ligaments. Every meal leads to later pain, as the nervous system shuts down blood flow, affecting the contractions of your digestive muscles, and decreases secretions needed for digestion. The stress can increase the acid in your stomach causing indigestion.

He suffers from paranoia and is afraid in almost every situation. He believes everyone is out to hurt him. He rehearses blistering speeches where he resigns and walks out. His inability to receive love worsens as he withdraws from family and friends.

When a person is under extreme stress their resistance to addictive behavior is impaired. Drugs only suppress the problem not solve the issues. Some retreat into video games or become obsessed with television. Others may be compulsively drawn to pornography or drink compulsively. They become open to all forms of physical and chemical abuse and as they lose their perspective of people, they begin to see them only as objects.

Ministry To Stage III

Job had a group of so-called comforters who just made

the situation worse. Do not become like them. Deliverance is not the solution. Spirits of oppression are not the problem. Spirits may contribute to the problem, but they are not the root. The root of the problem is the person's conduct.

- It may do more harm than good to tell him God loves him. He is convinced that the evidence points to the fact that God does not love him. Tell him that you love him. He may not believe it, but it is more tangible than the love of a God he can neither see nor any longer feel. It will then be your responsibility to prove that you mean what you say by not failing him.

- Respect his fences and withdrawal.

- Don't tell him to praise God for all things. His best approach to God is an honest cry of rage. When you can't praise God, be honest; call Him names; He'll probably fall off the throne laughing.

- It is best to pray for him is from a distance. Listen and be available.

- Love him in ways that do not demand a response.

- Listen, be available.

- At the appropriate time you may be able to speak the truth to him in love. The timing must be right and led by the Holy Spirit.

Avoiding Burnout

While others may minister to us when we are in burn out, it is best to avoid burn out whenever possible. The following steps are necessary to avoid burn out:

- Understand what God has called you to do and separate that from things that you believe you should do out of guilt.

- Protect your boundaries.

- Take a Sabbath day each week.

- Establish a time and place for your quiet time, away from all distractions.

- Realize your limitations.

- Listen to your body.

3. Job Description

With all of the demands upon a church pastors or ministers, how can they keep from burning out and maintain a healthy relationship with God, their family, and their congregation? The late theologian and minister, Henri Nouwen,[17] explains that when the task is so large there will be two opposite reactions: you jump in, work hard, and do everything you can until you totally burn out and give up, or you throw up your hands and do nothing. We have all witnessed both of these reactions by ministers over the years. To paraphrase Nouwen, there is a third alternative which will bring peace and satisfaction to the minister: discover which piece of the task you are called to accomplish, and do that well.

In the Jerusalem church a conflict arose when the needs of the Hellenistic believers were not being handled properly. There arose a faction that complained that the apostles were not meeting the needs of the people. The twelve apostles fell back on their job description.

Acts 6:2 (NIV) So the Twelve gathered all the

disciples together and said, "It would not be right for us to neglect the ministry of the word of God in order to wait on tables."

It was a matter of priorities for the apostles. With several thousand people in the church at that time, their call was to minister the word, not take care of all the details of running a church. As we see later in Acts, the ones chosen were not just serving food they were the leaders of the church. Stephen was stoned to death and it was not for waiting on tables. Phillip was a missionary and evangelist to Samaria, the Ethiopian Eunuch, and Caesarea. They moved in the power of the Holy Spirit.

It is important to understand the true purpose of our call. Leadership expert and former pastor, John Maxwell, once used a simple demonstration to make this point. Getting two volunteers, John explained to them that they were fireman. They were at the firehouse and he asked one to pantomime shining the fire pole and the other to simulate washing the fire engine. He watched as they acted out their tasks. In a few minutes they were asked what their job was. The first announced his job was to shine the fire pole, while the other responded that his job was to wash the fire engine.

"No!" Maxwell responded, "You are firemen; your job is to put out fires."

Too often we are so wrapped up in the details of the business of ministry that we forget our real task.

Each minister must know what his job description will be, whether it is officially written down somewhere or whether it is only in the mind of the minister. The job description must be based upon the minister's gifts, graces and priorities, not on the expectations of others.

Several years ago as I was moving into another phase of my ministry; the church asked me to provide them with a job description they could use when they called a new pastor. The following is part of what I provided.

Provide Spiritual leadership

Spiritual leadership is provided by leaders who are good examples of what they are trying to provide to others. Therefore, the Pastor should spend much of his time growing spiritually. This includes prayer, times away for meditation and communion with God, reading and studying the Bible for personal application, not just for sermon preparation.

He should also be a part of an on-going prayer group

for support, accountability, and mutual ministry. This should include a local and/or area pastors' groups. As the pastor grows spiritually, only then can he help the body to grow spiritually.

Teach the word of God.

The pastor should be well grounded in the Bible and in sound doctrine. He must be able to teach others.

Equip the body for ministry

Ephes. 4:11-12 (NIV) It was he who gave some to be apostles, some to be prophets, some to be evangelists, and some to be pastors and teachers, [12] to prepare God's people for works of service, so that the body of Christ may be built up.

The ministry of the church is to be accomplished by everyone in the body. It is the pastor's role to not only equip the body to minister, but also to provide opportunities for ministry. Equipping should include training, discipling, and releasing people into ministry. When people are equipped, the church's ministry will be multiplied.

Giftedness.

Not all pastors have the same gifting. Therefore it is not appropriate to expect a pastor to work effectively outside of his gifting. Some gifts are more suitable for shepherds than others. Encouraging, healing, mercy and giving of oneself are more pastoral gifts while prophecy may not be pastoral. It is difficult to be a prophet and a pastor at the same time.

Manage the resources of the church

The resources of the church include the time, the talents and gifts of each member and the church's property and finances. It should be the pastor's responsibility to assure that all of the church's resources are used in the best manner to further the Kingdom of God.

Guard the Flock

The position of pastor is not a job you take on because the hours are good or you can get rich. Being a pastor means laying down your life for the church. The pastor exists for the church in the same way as the shepherd exists to care for the sheep. He is to lay down his life for them as Christ did for the church. He must warn them when they are in danger; he must defend them against the enemy, Satan, and he must care for them. He must pray for them and fight spiritual battles for them.

A pastor's role is to strengthen the weak, heal the sick, take care of the flock, and search for the lost.

4. Conflict Resolution.

Conflict is unavoidable. Where ever there is movement there will be friction. But often we are fearful of confronting people. We are afraid they won't like us; we will be misunderstood; we may be rejected; we may make things worse. We fear the unknown, are not used to sharing our feelings, and we lack the needed skills in confronting others. But, how we handle conflict will determine our success in life. Some wrong ways to handle conflict include:

- Determine who is the most powerful. This results in a destructive power contest

- Determine who is right. Rights are frequently not clear, or the parties have differing perceptions of the standard. Sometimes different rules apply to the same situation. Sometimes contradictory standards apply.

Here are some bad ways to handle conflict:

- The "winner - take – all" method; shoot out at the OK corral.

- Walk away from it; peace at any price ignoring

its significance,

- Hear no evil - see no evil
- Whine about it, "Nobody knows the trouble I see."
- Wade around it; tiptoe through the tulips.
- Keep score; "It's my turn to win."
- White flag; yell, "Uncle"
- Blame someone else; "he said, she said"
- Use position, rank and serial number
- Hire a hit man; the Al Capone remedy

"On a given day ¾ of all churches' ministry is significantly reduced because of non-productive and destructive conflict." Lyle Schaller[18]

Causes of Conflict.

There are several causes for conflict.

- It is human nature. Cain had a problem with God and he took it out on his brother.
- Divisive people: No matter where they are, they sow discord.
- Hurting people. Hurting people hurt people. When a conflict begins the first thing to ask is,

"Is that a hurting person?"

- Political people. Controlling people usually cause conflict.
- Poor leadership. Sometimes the leaders cause conflict, and many times add to it. They keep the pot stirred.

"Ten Commandments" of Conflict Resolution

1. <u>Know the stages of conflict.</u>

There will be a downward spiral when the conflict goes unresolved.

   a. Remedy stage - fix the problem. Characteristics of this stage;
      o recognizing that there is a problem,
      o a disagreement of how to solve the problem,
      o a commitment to solve it,
      o and a belief it can be solved.
      o This stage requires honest communication.

   b. Re-positioning Stage. The characteristics of this stage are:
      o The focus shifts from solving the

problem to protecting oneself.

o People become nervous;

o they begin to generalize everything,

o and the trust level is low.

o Communication becomes cautious.

c. Rights Stage" - people declare their rights. "I am right, so you must be wrong." The characteristics of this stage are:

o People take sides, they become labeled,

o the solution shifts from solving the problem to winning. Whoever gets the biggest team will prevail.

o Communication is now overstated and distorted.

d. Removal Stage - "get rid of those people." The characteristics of this stage are:

o People are no longer satisfied with getting their own way, now they have to get rid of the opposition; the goal is divorce.

- o People are now in different camps and there is a clear leader in each camp.
- o Trust is gone.

e. Revenge Stage - "Make someone pay." The characteristics of this stage are:

- o People are not satisfied with a resignation,
- o People become fanatics,
- o The conflict has become a personal god issue.
- o They feel it is immoral to stop fighting.
- o The conflict goes out of bounds.

2. <u>Understand the goals of confrontation.</u>

A better understanding of what is to be achieved by confrontation is often required. Why do we need to confront a situation? We want to have a positive change or we want to have a growing relationship with them and that growth is hindered by the conflict.

When I am getting ready to reason with a

man, I spend one-third of my time thinking about myself and what I am going to say - and two-thirds thinking about him and what he is going to say. [Abraham Lincoln]

3. <u>Look at yourself</u>

Coping with difficult people is always a problem, especially if the difficult person is you.

4. <u>Look at the other person.</u>

5. <u>Meet together as soon as possible.</u>

Ephes. 4:26-27 "in your anger do not sin": do not let the sun go down while you are still angry, [27] and do not give the devil a foothold.

Do not "gunny sack" it. Don't get historical (Do not bring up the past). When conflict arises we are tempted to avoid it, procrastinate, ask someone else to handle it, or rationalize it.

6. <u>Outline the issue</u>

Describe what you perceive the other person is doing to cause the issue. Tell him/her how this makes you feel. Tell why this is important to you. What then are WE going to do to fix it.

7. Encourage a response

The people affected are going to feel shock, bitterness and resentment. They may not spare your feelings. Whatever they say or keep to themselves-they won't be ready to listen to the reason this is happening to them until they have expressed their emotions or had time to swallow their hurt. When confronting a person about a problem it is typical that half do not realize there is a problem, a third realize there is a problem but don't know how to solve it, and one fifth realize there is a problem, but don't want to solve it.

8. Speak the truth with love and gentleness

Unsolvable conflict is almost always because of a wrong attitude and not because of the issue. There are three types of people: hiders - they don't share the truth; hurlers throw a grenade - they share the truth, but not in love, and healers -they share the truth in love.

9. <u>Write down the desired action to be taken with the focus on the future.</u>

    The action plan should include

    - The issue

    - An agreement to solve the issue

    - Concrete ways that demonstrate the issue has been solved

    - An accountability structure to deal with the issue

    - A time frame to revisit the issue

    - A commitment by both sides to put the issue in the past once it is solved

10. <u>Reconciling interests and values.</u>

    Interests are needs, values, concerns, fears and desires. The things we care about are behind our position. Our position in a conflict is something we have decided upon and it is our interests that have caused us to make that decision. Reconciling interests, rather than positions, works for two reasons. For every interest, there are several possible positions that could satisfy it.

Behind opposing positions are more compatible interests than conflicting ones.

Manage Conflict Constructively

Constructive conflict management entails agreeing to a time and place to talk it out, honestly expressing your feelings, not personalizing the issue, focusing on the problem – not the person, selecting a neutral referee, and developing a positive mature attitude. Search for a solution, focus on specifics, and simplify the situation. Be open and available. When problems arise, work them out, listen, wait, and learn to forgive.

Destructive conflict management includes:

- Catching the other person off guard;
- Assertively, passively suppressing your feelings;
- Personalizing the disagreement;
- Getting your friends to referee;
- Being negative and as vindictive as possible.
- Finding someone to blame when something goes wrong,
- Generalizing and exaggerating what you consider to be the other person's wrongs, and

being silent and acting superior.

- Walking out, presuming, assuming, dominating, and stubbornly demanding guarantees when problems arise are destructive as well.

All of these attitudes will fuel the downward spiral of conflict.

5. Forgiveness

For a Christian, forgiving is not an option; it is a necessity (Matthew 6:14 – 15; Matthew 18:32-35). Christians cannot afford the luxury of even one small grudge. A grudge is like sand thrown in a well oiled machine. It steals our health, our joy, and our relationships - with God and other people. To paraphrase Matthew in the Scriptures above,

"God will forgive us to the extent that we forgive others." If God has not forgiven us, then we do not have a relationship with Him.

We may say a quick, "I forgive you," but forgiveness may not reach our heart. True forgiveness is in the heart, our innermost being. We may say the words of forgiveness, but if they do not touch our heart, we will remain angry and bitter. This anger and bitterness will remain lodged in the heart.

We may say, "No problem; its ok." But is it really ok? Our heart knows better as we continue to hold on to that grudge. This hurt will try to arise, but we will stuff it back down because, "We have forgiven." Then suddenly something will trigger a reaction which is way out of proportion to the incident or something that someone does or says. We get upset and wonder why. Often we do not really know why we are angry. This anger from the past will infect our current attitude and cause us problems until the past issues are resolved through true forgiveness.

We can use our present problems as a clue to unresolved issues of the past. When we react in ways incongruously a present situation, it is a tip off that there is something else bothering us. Where there is fruit, there is a root. Present problems can be symptoms of hidden bitter roots. How do you know if you have unforgiveness lodged in your heart?

Look at your present problems:

- Impairments to health.
- Chronic illnesses with no physiological diagnosis.
- Unwarranted anger
- Certain types of people you do not like without an apparent reason
- You just meet a person and realize immediately a strong dislike for them.

All of these may be the result of unforgiveness. This

can be fruit of a hidden root of bitterness.

If you wonder whether you have truly forgiven someone ask yourself these questions:

- When you see that someone coming towards you, do you cross the street rather than face him?
- Would you cross the street to see him?
- When you think about that person do you want to be his friend?
- Does your spirit desire relationship or do you want to flee?
- Are there certain people you cannot tolerate?
- Is there one of your children who really gets under your skin?

If you answer, "Yes," to any of these questions, pray and ask the Lord if there is someone you need to forgive.

My son and I had a traumatic relationship in his early teens. One day after the Lord showed me areas where I had hurt my son; I asked for and received his forgiveness. But there was one question for which he needed an answer, "Why were you so much harder on me than you were on my sister?"

He was right; I had been very hard on him, but why? The answer came after a soul searching prayer. The root cause was my son reminded me of myself. While learning to forgive others, I had never forgiven myself for the stupid things I had done when I was growing up. This unforgiveness of myself was the bitter root which affected my relationship with my son. It took some doing, but after a while, I was able to forgive myself and my relationship with my son was radically changed and became normal.

When anger and bitterness become lodged in the heart, you cannot forgive. Only Jesus can cleanse the heart.

Hebrews 10:22 let us draw near to God with a sincere heart in full assurance of faith, having our hearts sprinkled to cleanse us from a guilty conscience and having our bodies washed with pure water.

When you have been deeply hurt by someone or something, do not excuse it or wash it away. Do not stuff it. Acknowledge that you were hurt and that hurt is still there. When something is rooted in your heart, no simple, "I forgive you," will suffice. True forgiveness can only come when we work through three distinct steps:

Step 1

The first step in our prayer to forgive is to understand our own sinfulness. While we may feel we had no fault in the events that we must forgive, we need to realize that we are not sinless. We must lay aside our own self righteousness and admit we also have made and will make mistakes. In the Garden of Gethsemane, Jesus accepted the Father's purpose for Him - laying aside His righteousness and taking on the sins of all mankind.

> *2 Cor 5:21 God made him who had no sin to be sin for us, so that in him we might become the righteousness of God.*

Just as Jesus became our sin, we need to pray,

> *"Lord, help me to understand that I too have sinned. And as a sinner I lay my sins at the foot of the cross along with the one who hurt me."*

Our first task of prayer is to rediscover our oneness with the sin of mankind. Isaiah confessed:

> *"Woe to me!" I cried. "I am ruined! For I am a man of unclean lips, and I live among a people of unclean lips, and my eyes have seen the King, the LORD*

Almighty." Isaiah 6:5 (NIV)

If we go deep enough, we may see that our bitter root may have caused our brother to hurt us. We often want to run to the cross with our hurts, without acknowledging our own situation. If we do not lose our self righteousness and identify with mankind's sin, we will never be free. If not, we put on our "Martyr" hat, and say, "I forgave them." Then each time we forgive, we will feel more like a martyr.

When we are tempted to cry out, "I'm tired, I can't forgive anymore, I'm done, I won't," forgiveness was never complete. We are still high on our pedestal. We need to begin our prayers to forgive

> *"God, take me with you to Gethsemane until all those lines of who is right and who is wrong are lost in the sense of common shame at the foot of the cross."*

Behind all our hurt is that sneaky thought, "Wonderful me, I didn't deserve that kind of treatment." Instead, we should pray, "Oh God, forgive me."

Step Two

In step two, we have to accept the fact that Jesus took our sins to the cross. We should get to the point where we are so wounded that we realize we cannot forgive anyone at any time.

- Forgiveness is impossible for human flesh. Our feelings can fool us.

Jer 17:9 The heart is deceitful above all things and beyond cure. Who can understand it?

- No man is capable of forgiveness. We cannot force our heart to change.

Jer 13:23 Can the Ethiopian change his skin or the leopard its spots? Neither can you do good who are accustomed to doing evil.

- Only Jesus can enter the human heart and change it.

John 14:6 Jesus answered, "I am the way and the truth and the life. No one comes to the Father except through me.

- Sin and resentment separate us, but the blood of Jesus cleanses us from all.

1 John 1:9 If we confess our sins, He is faithful and just and will forgive us our sins and purify us from all unrighteousness.

Once we are in a position to receive God's gift of forgiveness, we simply receive by faith that Jesus has accomplished forgiveness for us. If we think we can forgive, we are not in a position to receive; we haven't died to our self-righteous forgiving self. When you come through Gethsemane, you know that neither the one who hurt you nor you, yourself, deserve forgiveness.

We claim by faith that forgiveness is accomplished. If we still grit our teeth when we see that person or find ourselves not liking him, it is not that forgiveness did not happen; it is that we were robbed of it because we did not go through Gethsemane to the foot of the cross with our brother. Forgiveness is still not complete.

Step Three

1 Peter 3:9 Do not repay evil with evil or insult with insult, but with blessing, because to this you were called so that you may inherit a blessing.

We are commanded to bless those who hurt us. That means we are to pray for all manner of good things to happen to them. We are to invest ourselves in love for his benefit.

- Bless those who persecute you[19]; bless and do

not curse.

- Rejoice with those who rejoice; mourn with those who mourn.
- Live in harmony with one another.
- Do not be proud, but be willing to associate with people of low position.
- Do not be conceited.
- Do not repay anyone evil for evil.
- Be careful to do what is right in the eyes of everybody.
- If it is possible, as far as it depends on you, live at peace with everyone.
- Do not take revenge, my friends, but leave room for God's wrath, for it is written:

"It is mine to avenge; I will repay," says the Lord.
On the contrary: "If your enemy is hungry, feed him;
if he is thirsty, give him something to drink. In doing
this, you will heap burning coals on his head." Do
not be overcome by evil, but overcome evil with good[20].

When God wants to reach a man who will not listen, He may cause him to hurt a Christian. That will plunge the Christian through Gethsemane to the cross for himself and pray for and bless the one who hurt him. This could build a bridge for the wounder to come into God's kingdom. As Stephen was being stoned to death he prayed for his killers:

"Lord, do not hold this sin against them." When he had said this, he fell asleep. The blood of the martyrs has always been the seed of the church. Acts 7:60 (NIV)

Standing nearby was Saul, a Jewish leader who was bent on destroying the "Way." Stephen's prayer may have established that bridge culminating in the one we know as Paul becoming an apostle of Jesus Christ. Blessing those who hurt you is not just a nice option; it is an absolute necessity if we are to be whole. Again, in the flesh, it is not possible.

If we do not want to, if it is not natural, then we have an unmistakable sign that the first steps of repentance in Gethsemane and restful receiving at the cross have not been accomplished in our hearts.

Sometimes much of this has to be accomplished away from the other person, but sometimes the Lord will require that we go to him and talk. Perhaps we are timid, afraid or unsure. If our fear is greater than the promptings of love, we have not prayed and acted it through to completion. Our brother needs to hear our forgiveness, our love and our blessing. Wisdom should prevent insensitive boldness in sharing, but fear and unworthy motives should not stop us.

It is humbling to go and speak words of forgiveness and blessing, and more humiliating to ask the one who hurt you for forgiveness for your role. But there is no easy option.

Failure to complete the process of forgiveness leaves unfinished business which causes further hurts and isolation. If the situation is not resolved, the debt has not paid, and we are back in prison.

When someone has died, you cannot go to them, but you can ask Jesus to communicate your forgiveness to them.

Eph5:21 Submit yourselves to one another out of reverence for Christ.

To summarize our path to true forgiveness:

1. First we must lose your self-righteousness and realize we too are sinners.
2. Then we must receive our forgiveness at the cross of Jesus.
3. Next we are to fulfill the Lord's direction to bless those who have hurt you.

4. When possible we could go to them to restore the relationship. There are times when circumstances are such as to make this impractical.

God's Immutable Laws

When God created the world, He set up absolute unchangeable laws. These laws were not established to keep us in check nor because God was angry. God's laws are for our benefit. Obedience results in happiness while disobedience can lead to catastrophe.

Gravity:

It does not matter if you believe in gravity or not. When we drop a ball it falls. It does not matter whether we believe in gravity. If I drop a dish it will fall and break whether or not we care about gravity. It doesn't mean that God hates the dish; it just broke because I let it go and gravity took over.

Action/Reaction:

Isaac Newton discovered that for every action there is an equal and opposite reaction. This is another powerful law. If I throw the ball at the wall, it will bounce back.

Balance

The world has been established to always be in balance.

If it is not in balance things will adjust to bring it into balance. In chemistry and mathematics we find that all formulae and equations must be in balance. Knowns and variables on one side must equal those on the other. When things are out of balance cataclysmic events occur. Have you ever been high in the air on a teeter totter when the other person got off? Balance has been eliminated and someone can get hurt.

We have come to accept the laws of nature and science. As we progress in our understanding of God's physical laws we send spacecraft to Neptune, land men on the moon, and travel around the world in airplanes constructed of all kinds of materials never known in years past.

But too often we think we can disregard God's spiritual laws without facing the consequences. Just as God set the natural/physical laws in place, He also set in place spiritual laws. If we understand the consequences of violating physical it is the same with God's spiritual laws. Everyone must understand the consequences of violating the spiritual laws God set in place. The Bible contains all of these spiritual laws along with the consequences of our disobedience. Laws are absolutes, yet the world thinks they can treat them as if they are opinions. We will look at three examples:

Honor your parents:

Deut.5:16 "Honor your father and your mother, as the Lord your God has commanded you, so that you may live long and that it may go well with you in the land the Lord your God is giving you.

Life will go well for you in every area in which we could in fact honor our parents. The corollary of that law is: life will not go well for us in every area in which we do not honor them. God loves us but also knows that if we break the law we can be hurt.

Carole came to us at a healing service. She and her husband were having serious problems. It looked like divorce was inevitable, because they had been getting further and further apart. We were led to ask her about her relationship with her father, who had recently been seriously ill. He had never shown any love for her at all and spent most of his time away from home. And her mother also was not a loving person. Carole was not able to honor her mother and father and as a result she was having problems in the same areas where she could not honor them - lack of love. This had affected her marriage.

Judge Not

Matt 7:1-2, "Do not judge, or you too will be judged. For in the same way you judge others, you will be judged, and with the measure you use, it will be measured to you." "Why do you look at the speck of sawdust in your brother's eye and pay no attention to the plank in your own eye? How can you say to your brother, 'Let me take the speck out of your eye,' when all the time there is a plank in your own eye? You hypocrite, first take the plank out of your own eye, and then you will see clearly to remove the speck from your brother's eye.

We will suffer in our lives in the same areas in which we have judged others.

Rom.2:1 "You, therefore, have no excuse, you who pass judgment on someone else, for at whatever point you judge the other, you are condemning yourself, because you who pass judgment do the same things."

Those things that offend us about others are usually those things where we have problems.

Sowing and Reaping

GAL 6:7 Do not be deceived: God cannot be and mocked. A man reaps what he sows.

This spiritual law is similar to the physical law of balance. If we sow love we will reap love and receive blessing. If we sow hatred, we reap destruction. As children, we sin and don't know it. We reap it later as adults. A corollary of sowing and reaping is the law of multiplication. As we sow, so will we reap but it will increase. Jesus was angry at the person who buried his talents. We are told to lay up treasures in heaven not on earth. God made the law of increase and sowing and reaping so we could sow good deeds and receive blessings. That was before sin entered the world. When sin entered, then the same laws of sowing, reaping, and multiplication applied, but if we sow evil we reap destruction. The more we sin, the worse it gets. It then is impossible to get away from sin. We become callous to sin.

C S Lewis writes in Mere Christianity how Hitler hated the Jews, so he persecuted them; the more he persecuted them the more he hated them until he was trying to wipe out an entire race. Love can increase the same as hatred. Keep doing the things you would do if you loved someone. It is not God's desire to punish His children. But if we violate a law there are consequences, not caused by God, but as a result of our violation of the laws.

Whenever we judge someone we set in motion a law. The result of which is we will do to others those things for which we condemn or blame them. Jesus became us so He could reap our sin. [21] Only if He became our sin could He reap our judgment. We must bring to death, the bitter root judgment.

We can backtrack from the fruit to find the root. Where there is the fruit of inordinate anger there will be a root cause. To find the root we can ask the Lord to help us find the root, and then the Holy Spirit directs the digging. If you say your husband never listens to you, tell me what your father was like. Did he show you affection, was he home a lot. Your wife often seems sicker than she actually is. How was your mother's health?

If there is fruit in our life that we want to get rid of we need to find out if it is due to bitter root judgment. Is there someone with whom we have a problem that shows similar behavior? Maybe we have judged him.

Once we have identified the root, we can pray for forgiveness for judging and ask Jesus to set you free from the consequences of that bitter root judgment.

> HEB.12:15 *"See to it that no one misses the grace of God and that no bitter root grows up to cause trouble and defile many."*

Bitter root judgment is an attitude of the heart, which becomes a bitter attitude of the mind. God spoke the world into existence. We speak blessings and curses on ourselves and others.

> *"I will never be like my mother." "I'll always be stupid, - .ugly,- clumsy, - etc." "I would never do that" "No none will ever love me."*

6. Judgement Begins In the House of the Lord

1 Peter 4:17 (NKJV) For the time has come for judgment to begin at the house of God; and if it begins with us first, what will be the end of those who do not obey the gospel of God?

Over the past few years we have witnessed a growth of sin within our leaders in the church. Apparently there have been serious problems for many years as the sex abuse scandals in the Roman Catholic Church attest. What is different now is the exposure of these issues in unprecedented numbers. No longer are church leaders able to hide their sin.

In the book of Acts, judgment came upon Ananias and Sapphira when they lied to the Holy Spirit.[22] In these days, sexual sin, and not lying, seems to lead the list. It may be that the church seems to react emotionally to sexual sin while looking the other way at lying, cheating, and chemical abuse.

Adultery

One of the more common problems faced by ministry

families is the pastor becoming involved an associate, a member of their congregation or support staff. This often leads to divorce, but sometimes the faithful spouse forgives and they stay together. We have witnessed several incidents where affairs are discovered which destroy the churches' trust in their leaders who are then removed for cause. While the church is still suffering, the leader divorces his wife and marries the woman with whom he had the affair. He then feels he has atoned and expects to be restored. We have known some that become serial adulterers repeating the sequence many times.

While living in the Pacific Northwest, I was in the ordination process. My mentor was a kind, loving, and spirit filled man nearing retirement. His maturity and love allowed him to speak his mind clearly to those around him. We met bi-weekly – usually on Wednesdays - to encourage, share concerns, needs, and just chat about our lives. Being in a small peer group on a regular basis for encouragement, advice, accountability, and fellowship is required by everyone in caring ministries. While the members of the group may change, its purpose remains intact, keeping you from going off the deep end and being a safe place to share needs.

One Wednesday my kind and gentle mentor was angry and frustrated. He explained, "Each Wednesday morning I meet for breakfast with two other pastors. We fellowship, share our needs, and pray for each other. We have been doing this together for four years."

His eyes became sad as he continued, "This morning one of the group called to say he would not be able to make it. A man had threatened to kill him and the police had advised him to stay out of sight. He continued, "It seems this pastor was having an affair with his secretary and her husband had just found out."

The predatory actions of the pastor was a shock as there had not been any clue dropped during four years of close relationship and breakfast prayer times. The three had become close over the years; encouraging each other, sharing needs and concerns. There had been no hint of any sexual misconduct. Later it came out that this was not the first time this pastor had an affair with someone in his church. It had been a continuing pattern. Each time he was caught his wife forgave him and the denominational leaders reassigned him to different church.

When the news of the pastor's infidelity became

common knowledge around the area churches, one pastor came up to me and told me a story that ended with his remark about infidelity, "There, but for the grace of God go I."

New denominational leadership began a time of "cleaning the house of God." Instead of covering up sexual misconduct by pastors, action was taken that fit the offense. In less than six months thirteen pastors lost their credentials and were removed from ministry. Many others were reprimanded and suspended.

At the time all of this was happening, we were on staff at a conference that focused on prayer and healing that was attended by many pastors. As we prepared workshops for this conference we felt led to develop a workshop which would help pastors and church leaders avoid the issues which lead to moral failure and bring healing to those involved. This workshop became one of the most attended and Rita and I have repeated it at several different venues throughout the region.

Why do so many Christian leaders fall into adultery? Noted Christian pastor, counselor, and teacher John Sandford[23] lists four issues which are potential causes of adultery to many in ministry; spiritual adultery, defilement, attachments, and transferences.

Spiritual Adultery

"Spiritual Adultery," according to Sandford, "*....occurs whenever one shares your deep feelings (worries, anxieties, and grief's); with someone else before you share them with your spouse. Deep feelings should always be shared first with your spouse. Problems arise when, in the course of sharing, we give that position of being our primary comforter to another. Only our spouse should hold that position. Husbands and wives refresh, comfort, and protect each other's heart. When we let some other person, man or woman, refresh our heart we are in Spiritual Adultery.*[24]"

It is not the problem of sharing. The problem comes when we share with someone other than our spouse those things that should be shared first or only with our spouse. God wants us, the Church, to move into intimacy, to really open up and share our hearts with one another. Unfortunately, as He is calling us into intimate, righteous sharing with one another, we are now less safe sharing than any other time in history. Most of us are not equipped to be intimate with one another without falling into sin.

God has called the church to a corporate-ness that

encourages us to share ourselves with others in the body of Christ. Small groups have become a popular means of incorporating new members into the body. People will relate to others at a much deeper level in a small group than could ever be experienced in the large worship setting. Most small group participants find that their relationship with God grows deeper as they experience a deeper relationship with other believers. People are encouraged to share their joys as well as their needs.

The problem is, "How do we learn to minister to each other and share on an intimate level as God is calling us to do in the Body, without falling into Spiritual Adultery?"

Rule number one is to have it together at home. Your spouse must be your primary comforter. If you are not married, you should share with a trusted family member or friend. We have advised many, "If you don't have it together at home then you need to stop ministering until you do get it together. "

John and Joan both had marriages which were going through difficult times. Both were strong believers and were seeking God on a deeper level. They never considered the possibility of entering into an affair, but they found themselves sharing a common bond of frustration. They both felt their respective spouses were slow to grow closer to the Lord. It began as they met and prayed for each other and prayed for their spouses. As their relationship grew, they began to share things with each other that they had never shared with their spouses. Most of their time together was spent at the church as John was on staff. Others in the church began to notice they were spending a lot of time together and warned them to be careful. They were quick to comment, "We are just ministering to each other."

In six months they both had filed for divorce from their spouses and had left the church. They later married and joined another church. Joan and John are fictitious names, but their story is not uncommon. This story represents how spiritual adultery leads to physical adultery.

People often ask me, "I am feeling that God is calling me into ministry. What do you think?"

My first response has been, "What does your spouse think about the idea?" Then my explanation, "Ministry is difficult, and without the support of a loving spouse to comfort and encourage you, your life will become difficult."

In 1984, I felt the Lord was calling me to become a full time Christian minister. My pastor and several respected friends all agreed that God was calling me. My wife Rita was definitely opposed to the idea. No matter how hard I could have argued, I knew it would be no use. The smartest thing I have ever done was to place this issue in the hands of the Lord in prayer, "Lord if you want me to become a pastor, you will have to convince Rita."

Five years later the Lord spoke to Rita. It happened on a two hour flight from our home in Washington State to California to teach at the annual Conference on Prayer and Healing in the San Bernardino Mountains. After landing at John Wayne Airport in Orange County, we picked up a rental car. Before we had left the airport grounds Rita asked, "How does a couple our age plant a church?"

Kiddingly, I asked her, "Why, do you want to be a pastor?"

"No. I want to be a pastor's wife." While reading a book on prayer, the Lord reminded Rita of her teenage desire to be a pastor's wife.

There are many married persons who feel called into

ministry and their spouse is against the idea. If they ignore the spouses concern, their ministries may not end well. If the minister is not able to share his ministry with his mate, he will seek others who understand. This can lead to spiritual adultery.

It is easy to insist that the Lord's call trumps any spousal objection, but I would question whether the Lord would call someone and not prepare the spouse. In many cases the spouse's objection may only be an indication that the timing is not right.

7. Attachments and Transferences

Anyone, Christian or not, can become infatuated or enamored with another and want to spend inordinate amounts of time with the other person. Attachments are most frequently "one way" relationships: from one who wants or needs something toward another who is thought to be able to provide it. The "love" in those cases is composed mainly of admiration and hope.[25]

There are several kinds of Attachments.

Friendship

We have all had the experience of meeting someone for the first time and realize that we are going to be deep friends or in other cases after continually running into someone over a period of time you become close friends. You begin to spend more and more time with them. We realize we want more to be more than acquaintances, we want a deeper relationship. Such a relationship developed between David and Saul's son Jonathon.

1 Samuel 18:1 (NKJV) [1] *Now when he had finished*

speaking to Saul, the soul of Jonathan was knit to the soul of David, and Jonathan loved him as his own soul.

A friendship attachment can be a great thing but it can become dangerous if it begins to move into spiritual adultery. Too much attention to friends could lead to idolatry as our friend may take the place of God in our lives.

Over the years some strange theologies have arisen in parts of the church based upon the concept of "Soul brother/sisters." The concept was to find your Soul Brother or Sister. Once found, the two could minister with an immediate increase joy, anointing, and power to minister. This Soul Brother/ Sister often were not the spouse. You can see the problems which can arise from this type of relationship. Husbands and wives are to be spiritual partners, no one else.

Attachments for Learning – Discipleship

Dave was a department manager in an engineering company. It was obvious that Dave was heading for bigger things. One young engineer decided to attach himself to Dave to learn and grow. Dave was willing and the relationship became mutual. They were inseparable at work. Later their relationship extended beyond the job to social and recreational activities. Dave played golf, smoked cigars, and drank Tanqueray Gin. His disciple followed suit. Dave switched to a pipe followed soon after by his shadow. As Dave was promoted and gained stature in the company, his prodigy followed along also gaining stature. This idolatrous all fell apart when Dave left the company and left a wounded disciple behind.

We all have our heroes whom we want to emulate. Discipling relationships can be Holy, valuable and profitable for both parties. We want to learn all they know. We want to be like them. But there is a warning. The relationship can become abusive when the discipler begins to use the disciple for his own personal gain. Often the disciple is either clueless or accepts the abuse for fear of losing the relationship.

God does not want us to become carbon copies of another and to give up our thinking for another man's thinking. So if you find someone and you latch on to learn, keep your own mind in the Lord.

Counselling or Prayer Attachments.

When counseling or praying for another, attachments

are common. The counselee sees the light of Jesus in the counselor and they want to latch on. When ministering to others, as a medical or spiritual professional we must fight our own tendency to be God to the person we are helping. While people in need a touch from someone with skin, it is important to keep them focused on the real God. As a minister we should be transparent so they get to Jesus through us, and not allow them to believe we are their savior. They need to attach themselves to the Lord, not the minister.

Secular counselors are often trained to be detached from their patient or client. Christian ministers, on the other hand, meet a person not only face to face, but also heart to heart. Statistics have shown that untrained prayer ministers may have better success in healing people than their professional counterparts. The prayer minister becomes close to the one with needs and can love that person back to life. When someone feels loved, they begin to have hope and as a result are able to change.

Ministry attachments are normally positive and a result of trust. However, medical and spiritual ministers must always be careful to prevent the attachments from becoming idolatrous. We must always get out of the way and make them aware that it is God, not the minister who should be worshipped.

> *And I fell at his feet to worship him. But he said to me, "See that you do not do that! I am your fellow servant, and of your brethren who have the testimony of Jesus. Worship God! For the testimony of Jesus is the spirit of prophecy.*[26]"

Transferences:

A transference is defined as an unconscious phenomenon in which the client projects onto the minister, nurse, or therapist attitudes, feelings, and desires originally linked with early significant persons. The care giver represents someone important in the client's past or current life. The counselee may love the counselor like a father, like a mother, brother, sister, lost friend etc. The counselee thinks he is in love with the counselor. It's not a real love, it's a projection.

Transference is always entered into from the weaker to the stronger. If you suspect transference in a professional relationship do not cut the person off. They will feel rejected which may not be easily handled. Instead talk it over. Talking about it will lift away the fear and guilt that they might feel. Sometimes they will not let you talk it out because they don't want to hear it's not a real love. You must hold the line in righteousness.

Warding off Attachments and Transferences

1. Clear yourself first through prayer. Pray, *"Lord, if there is anything in me that causes me need to be needed, if there is a hidden need for someone to fall in love with me, if there is a hidden need to punish myself or some one else; I bring all this to death on the cross."*

2. Ask yourself why am I not transparent? Why are they latching on to me?

3. Let God love them through you. Trust God. And they will go through you to the Lord.

4. If there is a root cause for you to be needed, pray especially for your need to be needed to die. *"Lord, put the cross between me and the counselee. Let there be a filtering of you between me and the person. So that they are relating to you first and then to me. Lord, you be there between us."*

8. Compassion fatigue

John [not his real name] moved into Minden, Louisiana town to become the pastor of a large denominational church. It was obvious to other church leaders that John would be a great asset to the community and the Ministerial Association as we worked to unite a divided city. At one time Minden had been a thriving industrial town in northwestern Louisiana. Over time the factories had either left or cut back operations and the city was in decline in population and morale. As a newcomer with a fresh set of eyes, and the authority of his position John felt that there were some specific actions that could be taken to turn the town around. His drive enabled the Ministerial Association to lead the development of a plan for the future of the city which was accepted by the local government, Chamber of Commerce, school board, and other interested agencies.

Then something happened to John. His initial excitement turned to hopelessness, his energy was gone, and he seemed to have lost interest in everything. Rumors had it that his wife was going to leave him.

John's church had an older congregation. At one point he confided in me that he had officiated at seven funerals in one month's time and that over one year there had been over twenty deaths and many more congregants in the hospital with serious health issues. John had become a victim of Compassion Fatigue.

On August 31, 1986 Aero México Flight 498 was clipped by a Piper Archer over Cerritos, California while descending into Los Angeles International Airport. All sixty seven people on both aircraft were killed and an additional fifteen people on the ground were also lost. One of the first responders was a local minister who spent days at the crash site ministering to the ground survivors and helping the fire and rescue workers. Compassion fatigue set in almost immediately. The next week this pastor had to leave his ministry. It was several years until he could be restored.

Compassion fatigue, also known as secondary traumatic stress (STS), is a condition characterized by a gradual lessening of compassion over time. It is common among individuals that work directly with trauma victims such as nurses, psychologists, pastors, and first responders. Ministering regularly to the needs of an aging and dying congregation can bring on STS.

It was first diagnosed in nurses in the 1950s. Sufferers can exhibit several symptoms including hopelessness, a decrease in experiences of pleasure, constant stress and anxiety, sleeplessness or nightmares, and a pervasive negative attitude. This can have detrimental effects on individuals, both professionally and personally, including a decrease in productivity, the inability to focus, and the development of new feelings of incompetency and self-doubt.

A few years ago I was diagnosed with Non-Hodgkin's lymphoma and was sent to Dr. Bobby Graham an oncologist and a very devout Christian. Friends who knew him told me that he was hard to see because he had to take regular times away from his practice. They explained that he saw so much disease and death that it weighed heavily on him. In order to maintain his perspective and give his patients his very best, he needed to get away regularly. Although I have been cancer free for several years I like to drop in on Dr. Graham as an encouragement to him that he has some success in his personal war against cancer.

Getting away or dropping out of ministry for a time are effective in curing Compassion Fatigue. To avoid it in the first place, the next chapter describes eight steps which caring ministers can practice.

9. Eight Steps to a Joyful Ministry.

Ministry is not for the faint of heart, but it is satisfying to lead people to physical, spiritual, and relational wholeness. The Greek word "sozo" means to make whole, heal, make well, restore, and save. It describes what we all do as ministers, health care providers, and mental health workers. It is an awesome honor to be called into this ministry. Despite the risks to their own health many continue to serve others and receive the internal rewards of doing good things.

There are eight specific actions which, if taken, will keep caregivers from falling into the traps that have caused others to leave their calling. John and Paula Sandford refer to these actions as "Spiritual Hygiene."

Stick to God's Call.

Many of us are quick to take on more responsibilities than God has assigned to us. We do this for many reasons; we want to be accommodating, we want others to like us, we want to feel important, or we feel that if we do not do them they will not be done. There are always many good things that need to be done that do not have our name on them. If we take on someone else's task we run the risk of overloading ourselves and robbing them of the blessing they would receive in serving.

Maintain Your Sabbath.

Exodus 20:8-10a (NKJV) [8] "Remember the Sabbath day, to keep it holy. [9] Six days you shall labor and do all your work, [10] but the seventh day is the Sabbath of the LORD your God. In it you shall do no work:

Highly driven people try to make every minute count. For them there is no Sabbath rest. Ministers, healthcare workers and first responders often are not able to take off on their normal Sabbath day. As a result many forego a day of rest. God created us to be cyclical in our work. It is important that we rest one day for every six that we work. If we forego our weekly day of rest, we become vulnerable to all types of physical relational and spiritual issues. When we take on more than what God has called us to we lose our sense of balance and with it our ability to think, reason, and take care of ourselves.

When someone calls and says "I will die if you can't see me today." You need to ask them "How long have you had this problem?" Most will respond that it has been going on for years, but they have to get it fixed right now. If they have waited for years to call they can wait until a more convenient time for you.

Physical Exercise

Physical exercise is one of the greatest relievers of stress we have available to us. According to the prestigious Mayo Clinic,

> *"Exercise in almost any form can act as a stress reliever. Being active can boost your feel-good endorphins and distract you from daily worries."*[27]

We all know that exercise is good for our bodies, but we are often too busy and stressed to fit it into your routine. Virtually any form of exercise can act as a stress reliever. If you're not an athlete or if you are out of shape, you can still make a little exercise go a long way toward stress management. Physical activity helps to increase the production of your brain's feel-good neurotransmitters, called endorphins. Regular exercise can increase your self-confidence and lower the symptoms associated with mild depression and anxiety. Exercise also can improve your sleep, which is often disrupted by stress, depression, and anxiety.

Take Time to Laugh

"Your sense of humor is one of the most powerful tools you have to make certain that your daily mood and emotional state support good health."[Paul E. McGhee, Ph.D.][28]

It is important to all who are in ministry to take time to laugh. Go see a funny movie. Do not be afraid to laugh at yourself. Be among people who have a good sense of humor. Laughter is a powerful antidote to stress, pain, and conflict. Nothing works faster or more dependably to bring your spirit, soul, and body back into balance than a good laugh. Humor lightens your burdens, inspires hopes, connects you to others, and keeps you grounded, focused, and alert.

- Laughter relaxes the whole body.
- Laughter boosts the immune system.
- Laughter triggers the release of endorphins.
- Laughter protects the heart.
- It improves the function of blood vessels and increases blood flow.

Take Time for Yourself.

My time for myself usually comes in the mornings.

These are times when I can be quiet before the Lord, read, study, meditate, and pray. For my wife Rita, painting gives great satisfaction, "I can move the paint around and if it doesn't look quite right, I can scrape it off." Take time for whatever it is that satisfies you. Let God bless you through it. Through these times, the Lord will equip you for His call and use it as a part of your protection.

Earlier in my life being alone was very threatening to me. When we are left alone we come face to face with our aloneness and are so afraid of loneliness that we will find anything to get busy again. We run away from loneliness and seek after distractions; we read another book, we go to another conference, listen to another tape, or find another fellowship.

> *Instead of running away from our loneliness and trying to forget or deny it, we have to Protect it and turn it into fruitful solitude. To live a spiritual life, we must find the courage to enter into the desert of our loneliness and change it by gentle and persistent efforts into a garden of solitude. This requires not only courage, but a strong faith.*[29]

Maintain Healthy Relationships.

Broken or damaged relationships suck the very heart out of you. Some relationships may not be restorable and in those cases we need to forgive. Sometimes forgiveness has to be a regular thing. Peter asked Jesus, "How many times are we to forgive?" Jesus responded with a number far beyond what anyone could have imagined.

Our relationships with those we encounter on a regular basis must be kept healthy. As mentioned in an earlier chapter, "If you do not have it together at home, you should seriously consider getting out of the ministry until you get it together."

Our relationships with fellow workers and other staff must be kept healthy our ministry and our personal life will suffer.

Maintain Your Devotional Life,

Our relationship with God must be intimate and healthy. How else will we be able to respond to His direction and call on our lives? How else will we know our assignment? We need to stop and listen and wait upon the Lord. He will speak to us and guide our life.

We must also be honest with Him about our desires and our feelings. Our prayers may not always courteous to God. But they should be honest. Tell Him exactly how you feel. He knows your heart anyway.

> *Jeremiah 20:7 (NKJV) [7] O LORD, You induced me, and I was persuaded; You are stronger than I, and have prevailed. I am in derision daily; Everyone mocks me.*

When I graduated from seminary, they gave me a gift of a little red book with Psalms and Proverbs. The book is arranged for a daily devotion covering an entire month. On the first day of the month you are to read Psalms, 1, 31, 61, 91, 121, and Proverbs 1. Then day 2 you read Psalms 2, 32, 62, 92, 122, and Proverbs 2. It continues in that way through the month. With each reading, there will be one or two verses which cause me to stop and meditate. When reading on the eleventh day I discovered my life calling.

> *O God, You have taught me from my youth; And to this day I declare Your wondrous works. Now also when I am old and gray-headed, O God, do not forsake me, Until I declare Your strength to this generation, Your power to everyone who is to come.*

[Psalm 71:17-18 (NKJV)]

Thank God

Thank God for all He has given you. Doctors say the healthiest emotion you can have is gratitude. In fact the more you work on this attitude of being grateful, the healthier you will be. Be thankful for everything you receive.

Each day find five things you that you are thankful for and express your gratitude to God.

10. Intercessory Prayer.

The normal life breath of every Christian is intercession. If Jesus lives in our heart we must constantly be in intercessory prayer. The very life breath of a Christian is intercession.

> *If we do not spend ourselves daily in intercession, the Lord may indeed be in our hearts but we are not allowing Him to live His life in us, because intercession is what He is always doing. [John Sandford]*

About five percent of all Christians have the spiritual gift of intercession, but all Christians are called into intercession. Intercession is distinctly different from other types of prayer. Other types of prayer usually begin in the heart or mind of the person; we want something and we petition God for it, we are grateful - so we praise Him, we are hurting - so we cry out to be comforted. Intercession is unique. Intercession always begins in the heart of God. Intercession is God's Holy Spirit brooding over His creation, as in the beginning, and finding that void and moving to fill it.

It is the one true prophet, God, seeing what is going to happen, and searching for someone to tap on the shoulder, and say, "Stand in the gap and call others, I don't want this to happen."

Intercession is necessary because of our free will. God could have created us to be robots, but He decided to give us free will. Before any illness hits, before any death approaches, before any accident looms, the Father waits to have compassion on us.

Isaiah 30:18 Yet the Lord longs to be gracious to you; he rises to show you compassion. For the Lord is a God of justice. Blessed are all who wait for him!

But He has given the earth and our lives into our care. He is careful not to do too much because it could rob us of the purpose of our lives. He restrains His loving desire when everything in Him wants to help. Just as we older parents want to step into our children's lives and help. It's as simple as when the neighbors next door are having problems. It is their problem. We do not want to get involved. But if they pick up the telephone and ask for help, we will go right over. It is the same with God, He wants to help, but He restrains Himself because it is our house.

Burden bearing intercession

Often intercession is objective and detached. God calls us to pray about something and we pray. We may not know what or who we are praying for. On our first trip to the Holy Land, I woke up in the middle of the night and prayed for over two hours. I did not know why. Later I began praying for a specific individual on the trip. Towards the end the Lord called me to intercede again. Sometimes we are to just pray at a distance and at other times we may be called to bear another's burdens.

At a healing service in San Diego a middle aged woman came to me for prayer. As she approached, there was a sudden pain in the back of my neck. It felt as if someone had hit the back of my neck with a two by four board. It was so real that it almost knocked me to the floor. It was the most intense pain I ever felt in my neck, and it lasted for several minutes while the woman shared her need. She did not want prayer for herself but was asking prayer for her son who was in construction and had fallen from a platform and broke his neck. As together we interceded for the young man, the pain in my neck began to ease.

Galatians 6:2 (NKJV) [2] *Bear one another's burdens,*

and so fulfill the law of Christ.

Burden Bearing is a supreme act of love. It is not an option but a command. It is one of the most effective forms of intercession. It is not objective and detached, burden bearing is having compassion and empathy - putting yourself in the others shoes and understanding where they are. God may call us to carry the burden for someone or something. We may physically feel something strange; we may feel tired, weak, or depressed. Sometimes we may even feel physical pain. These are often clues to the burdens for which we are to intercede. We do not ask God to give us someone else's pain or sickness so we can carry it for them. We cannot do that. Only Jesus is the burden-Bearer

> *Isaiah 53:5 (NKJV)* [5] *But He was wounded for our transgressions, He was bruised for our iniquities; The chastisement for our peace was upon Him, And by His stripes we are healed.*

As an intercessor, bearing burdens, we share with Jesus His ministry of healing. The intercessor does not hold on to the burden but passes it on to Jesus at the cross.

There are times when someone may be overwhelmed by their burdens. They may be mired down emotionally and not even able to pray. When that happens, God will send one of His prayer warriors. He reaches through to that person to identify with their hurting hearts. The Holy Spirit reaches through the intercessor to draw the hurts to the cross of Jesus. The burden bearer does not hold on to the burden but passes it through to Jesus.

Burden Bearing clears the static and tunes our radios to hear God better. It helps us minister to others whom we may be counseling. Burden bearing is the primary way in which God wants to call us to intercession. He sometimes allows us to sense some of the grief, fear, hurt, anger or whatever has been weighing someone down. We then are called to lay down our lives for others. Burden bearing involves an empathetic identification with the other person, a compassion for the person's needs. This is done by the Holy Spirit, not in our flesh. If we do it in our own flesh it profits nothing. This is not substitution, we may feel the pain but we pass that pain on to the Lord. We should pray:

> *"Lord Jesus, You come and draw his pain unto yourself. and I will share in your feelings if you do that."*

Jesus provides the model of burden bearing. In

Gethsemane He accepted the task of laying down His life for us. He bore our sin and laid down His relationship with the Father. He did this because of the law. He became us so he could become our sin.

> *2 Corinthians 5:21 (NKJV)* [21] *For He made Him who knew no sin to be sin for us, that we might become the righteousness of God in Him.*

He died not only physically, but heart mind and soul. He was no longer acceptable to the Father. When we become born anew we are washed clean. Then we can come into the Father's presence. That is the life we are called to lay down in burden bearing.

> *Romans 12:1 (NKJV)* [1] *I beseech you therefore, brethren, by the mercies of God, that you present your bodies a living sacrifice, holy, acceptable to God, which is your reasonable service.*

Our worship is laying down our life for others. If you want a revival, there must be great intercession for your leaders.

Seven Rewards of Burden Bearing.

Burden bearing is not an easy ministry. It is not something many people seek, but we are all called to bear one another's burdens. There are seven great rewards to bearing the burdens of others.

1. You die faster. We die to our own sins and we die to our self-righteousness. We become living sacrifices to the Lord.
2. You learn to hate sin.
3. You fall in love with Jesus all over again.

   2CO 4:10-11 We always carry around in our body the death of Jesus, so that the life of Jesus may also be revealed in our body. For we who are alive are always being given over to death for Jesus' sake, so that his life may be revealed in our mortal body.

   PHI 3:10 I want to know Christ and the power of his resurrection and the fellowship of sharing in his sufferings, becoming like him in his death, and so, somehow, to attain to the resurrection from the dead.

4. The Bible comes alive.
5. You experience repentance and death.
6. You receive a quickened conscience
7. You become intimate with God.

   JOH 14:21 Whoever has my commands and obeys

them, he is the one who loves me. He who loves me will be loved by my Father, and I too will love him and show myself to him."

JOH 14:23 Jesus replied, "If anyone loves me, he will obey my teaching. My Father will love him, and we will come to him and make our home with him.

EPH 3:14 For this reason I kneel before the Father,

The ministry of bearing the burdens of others is not a clean ministry. That is why it does not often happen in the Television church or those churches where the leaders are in control. It only happens where the Holy Spirit has His way.

There are serious dangers in burden bearing. We can be carried away by our empathetic nature. God has gifted us with the basic equipment to sense things in others. When we give ourselves to God, He uses those gifts. We need to discern whether it is within us or are we receiving something from God.

11.   Spiritual Hygiene

2 Corinthians 7:1 (NKJV) [1] *Therefore, having these promises, beloved, let us cleanse ourselves from all filthiness of the flesh and spirit, perfecting holiness in the fear of God.*

You Have Been Slimed

In the 1984 version of the movie Ghostbusters, Peter Venkman, played by Bill Murray, comes too close to a demonic green blob, and is slimed. Venkman ends up with green, sticky, viscose slime all over his body and uniform. The hilarious movie makes for good fantasy entertainment, but is it illustrating a real concept. Can we be slimed by being close to evil?

On my first trip to India, I became aware of a strange phenomenon. As I rode from the airport into the city of Mumbai, I felt an oppressive heaviness which I realized was not physical. It affected my emotions, but it was not an emotional reaction to what I was seeing. It did not make me fearful, but awakened me to be alert and be careful. Something was affecting my spirit. Occasionally the oppression would lift only to return within a few seconds. Over the next several days I detected a pattern to what I was feeling. In certain areas of the city the heaviness was overwhelming, while in others it lifted. Each time it lifted I looked around for some reason. Many times it lifted while driving past a Christian church. This was same thing I had sensed earlier Cairo, Egypt and Amman, Jordan.

We left Mumbai and took a regional airline to the city of Bangalore. As we deplaned, there was a surprising spiritual lightness. The sense of oppression had abated considerably. The next day while taking a break from my business meetings we walked through the streets and continued to feel almost joyful. The street children were still begging, the constant smell of polluted air was still prevalent, but it was different than Mumbai. Turning a corner we suddenly got our answer. A huge billboard atop a five story building announced a Christian revival that had begun earlier and was continuing that day. I can still remember the words on the billboard.

> *Are you having problems with your family?*
> *Are you having trouble with your job?*
> *Are you hurting and wounded?*
> *Come and meet my friend Jesus!*

We live in a world where pollutants affect our air and

water. In our highly technical world we are polluted by electromagnetic radiation, both manmade and natural. Do we also live in a spiritually polluted world? Yes we do.

In 1934, California Institute of Technology selected Mount Palomar in northern San Diego County for the Hale 200 inch telescope. Palomar was selected because of the clear skies and low level of ambient light. Since then population growth brought automobile headlight, street lights and security lights to the area below the mountain resulting in an increase in the level of background light. As a result the sensitivity of the observatory's telescope was significantly reduced. It lost its ability to see deeper into space.

With the backdrop of sin and evil in our world today, even devout Christians are becoming so desensitized that it becomes more difficult to realize the warnings of our spirit. Spiritual heaviness and oppression, no longer trigger a response. We are like the proverbial "Frog on the Kettle" that cannot sense a gradual heating of the pot until he is cooked.

Throughout the ages wise people have realized that we live in two worlds at the same time, a physical outer world, and an inner spiritual world. I prefer to use the term "spiritual environment" because it refers not only to something inside of us, but also to the spiritual world that exists around us. According to scripture we war against spiritual forces.

> *Ephesians 6:12 (NKJV)* [12] *For we do not wrestle against flesh and blood, but against principalities, against powers, against the rulers of the darkness of this age, against spiritual hosts of wickedness in the heavenly places.*

> *Romans 8:38-39 (NKJV)* [38] *For I am persuaded that neither death nor life, nor angels nor principalities nor powers, nor things present nor things to come,* [39] *nor height nor depth, nor any other created thing, shall be able to separate us from the love of God which is in Christ Jesus our Lord.*

Pierre Teilhard de Chardin[30], the visionary Jesuit priest, wrote in the 20th century:

"We are not human beings having a spiritual experience; we are spiritual beings having a human experience".

Human beings were created to live with the ability to touch two coexisting environments; spiritual and physical.

Doctors, nurses, and care givers see the worst in their patients, clients, and associates. Pastors, counselors, and prayer ministers often hear some of the most grotesque tales of man's inhumanity to man or woman. It is difficult to not be hardened to the evil around us. It is difficult to maintain our human sensitivity when all around us is evil. When Rita and I first began to regularly pray for people, we realized what a sheltered life we had led. As we prayed for physical healing, the Lord often led us to a look for a spiritual or emotional root to the physical ailment. Spiritual and emotional problems often manifest in physical ailments. This is not to say that the physical ailment was not real, but the root may have been non-physical. As we prayed we often would see the physical symptoms began abate, but would return a day or two later. When we were able to find the root of the problem - physical, spiritual, or emotional – the effectiveness of our prayer ministry increased dramatically. But with this success we opened ourselves to a disturbing reality; man's inhumanity to man. After many of these sessions, we would feel as if we had been slimed.

We all are familiar with the way hospitals are continuously fighting against infections. This is for the safety of patients and the health care workers. There are strict rules of Hygiene which are enforced. There are notable examples of poor hygienic practices that infected many.

While physical infections are well known, there are also spiritual infections which can spread spiritual disease. All persons involved in the healing ministries - body, soul and spirit, - need to practice spiritual hygiene. We are slimed by hearing stories of atrocities, and seeing the evidences of serious wounding. We must practice a form of spiritual hygiene in order for us to continue to be effective ministers.

Spiritual Shower

After a shift at the hospital, office, or church dealing with infective situations we will often become unclean. The first five books of the Old Testament, the Torah identify many things that make a person unclean and prescribe remedies such as ritual washing. When we have been slimed and are unclean it is time to take a spiritual shower. We may want to combine this with a physical shower.

First pray, "Lord, wash me clean, you are the Living Water. Wash away all of the junk that has come into me from ministry today. Wash me clean from all the gory details." We are washing away things that have stuck to our human spirit. We are not supposed to hold on to the burdens of others. God asks to minister to others in His power and authority and to pass all the pain and hurt up the line to Him. We become defiled as we hold on to what we should be passing through.

We need to also pray, "Lord, take this burden from me. Your burden is not oppressive but I have made it so."

Celebrate the Lord's presence

Before we enter into a hospital room, a patient encounter, or a ministry situation it is important to acknowledge that the Lord is with us. We can celebrate that presence in prayer. Pray that He will place Himself between you and your task and be a holy filter to protect you. His presence is a reality, not something we just put in our mind, but we choose to be aware of His presence as we meet with the patient, client, or parishioner.

Pray "Lord, don't let me think, do, say, feel, etc. anything that would dishonor You. Let me be in tune with You."

Cleanse the atmosphere

The spiritual pollution is all around us. Before we begin to minister we need to spiritually cleanse the area in which we are going to minister. This brings up the question, "Do we have spiritual authority to safely cleanse a place?" When we are ministering in an area where we have ownership, we have the authority. If we are ministering in an area where we have no authority, someone else's home, a hospital room, or a public place, it is more effective to pray and ask the Lord to cleanse the space.

Spiritual warfare is not chasing demons around, but taking the light of Christ into dark places. The intensity of our light is a function of our relationship with Christ. When we are closer to Him, our light shines brighter.

> *"Lord, we ask that you bring the light of your spirit into this place to replace the darkness.*

Take regular breaks from Ministry

My oncologist, a Christian, makes it a point to get away from his practice for long periods of time because he becomes slimed by the sickness and death that he sees on a daily basis. The heaviness and oppression around him disease and death suck the life out of a person. Although I am now cancer free, I return annually not for a checkup, but as an encouragement to my doctor that he is succeeding in his ministry to cancer patients.

For many years I looked down at monks who spent so much time alone in prayer and devotions, locked in a monastery away from people. In my immaturity, I felt they could better serve God ministering to God's people out in the streets. Then I read somewhere that you cannot really understand the needs of the world until you get away from it for a time. While we are in a spiritual environment with which we are familiar, we become desensitized to the needs of that environment. If we get away to a place of prayer and meditation, we will be able to hear God clearer and when we return to our place of ministry we are more sensitive to both good and evil.

12.   Wounded Spirit

"the infinite abyss can only be filled by an infinite and immutable object, that is to say, only by God Himself." [Blaise Pascal][31]

There is a God shaped (hole) vacuum in each of us that can only be filled by God, Himself. There is something within humans that wants to reach out to God. In order for this desire to be satisfied we must experience Him in close and intimate relationship. Philosophers and theologians may differ on the in terminology but all agree there is something beyond animal instincts that sets us apart from other species. In Christianity this deep inner place is our human spirit which is different from our soul. The writer of the letter to the Hebrews makes it clear there is a difference between our soul and our spirit.

Hebrews 4:12 (NKJV) For the word of God is living and powerful, and sharper than any two-edged sword, piercing even to the division of soul and spirit, and of joints and marrow, and is a discerner of the thoughts and intents of the heart.

Note that there is a very fine line between our soul and spirit which is difficult to define, But God's Word is living, powerful and sharp enough to make the distinction.

> *1 Thessalonians 5:23 (NKJV)* [23] *Now may the God of peace Himself sanctify you completely; and may your whole spirit, soul, and body be preserved blameless at the coming of our Lord Jesus Christ.*

Paul, in writing to the church in Thessalonica, prays that their whole body, soul, and spirit be sanctified. Again, Paul makes a distinction between soul and spirit.

If there is a spirit distinct from the soul what is its purpose? The first thing we realize is; the spirit is that part of us that seeks to have an intimate relationship with God. In their significant book, "Healing the Wounded Spirit[32]," John and Paula Sandford define the functions of the human spirit are to:

- Allow us to enter into Corporate worship
- Enable us to enjoy satisfying, personal devotions.
- Give us the ability to hear God.
- Enable us to be inspirational/rather than just following a routine.
- Give us the ability to transcend time.

- It provides us the ability to commune and communicate with ease, and enjoy an intimate relationship with our spouse.
- The human spirit provides a good conscience which works before we act impulsively.

We are all born with a live functioning Spirit. However, that spirit must be nurtured through warm physical affection. If a baby does not receive enough human touch in the first two years of life its spirit may never become active. It may be wounded or be dormant. As children grow, trauma in the forms of abuse, neglect, abandonment, sickness, or serious injury can wound the human spirit.

In 2003 we were asked to lead a workshop on "ministry to the abused" as part of a pastors and leaders conference in Bogota, Colombia. When we arrived we discovered a very high percentage of men and women had been sexually abused as a result of the drug traffic and revolutionary wars of the past few years. Many of these people were so wounded spiritually that they were unable to participate in church services and daily life. They seemed to just go around as if they were in a daze. The response to our workshop was overwhelming and we were asked to return with a specialized team to train pastors and leaders to deal with the wounded in their communities.

The following year our team ministered in Bogota, Medellin, and Santa Marta with great success. We used the Cross Current program from Andy Comiskey's Desert Streams Ministries[33] as a guide.

While Colombia was an extreme case, care givers of all types may have had their spirit wounded as a child or later in life. People who have suffered trauma and abuse often feel called to minister to those who have experienced similar trauma. In fact we find that God uses our bad experiences and difficulties to minister to others. As a minister or care giver, the odds are high that you have been hurt and may need healing and restoration yourself.

Wounding occurs as we become vulnerable to someone we trust, we begin to open up to them and our trust is violated. We get hurt. As a result we begin to build up walls to protect ourselves. We make vows that no one will ever hurt us again. We develop a heart of stone. These same walls that we use to protect ourselves become a jail. They keep us from being close to others. They separate us from God. They cause us to react to things in weird manners.

Identifying the Wounded Spirit.

If we look at the functions of the human spirit and ask ourselves how we rate ourselves we can evaluate the condition of our spirit. We all have a bit of wounding in our spirit, but for some it is so severe that it is difficult for them to function as a human being. Pastors, nurses, doctors, and other care givers are not immune. In fact these professions are most vulnerable. Because their role is to help people, they get their self-worth from how well their people fair. Every pastor I have ever met has been traumatized at least once by an upset parishioner.

A simple yes or no answer to the following questions will help identify any spiritual wounds. These questions are based upon the writings of John and Paula Sandford which we have found to accurately reflect the condition of the spirit.

1. When you are in worship or prayer, do you feel the presence of God flowing over you and through you, or do you only know he is there by faith?

   _____

2. In private devotions, do you enter into His presence? Can you stay in His presence? When you read the Bible do the words come alive with

meaning or does the Bible reading run dry?
_____

3. Do you ever hear the Lord or have spiritual dreams or visions? Does God speak to you? _____

4. When you are in conversation with others, do you enter in and feel what the other person feels, or do you just figure out with your mind, what to say?
_____

5. Are you a creative person? Do you have new ideas? Or do you always have to follow the instruction manual? _____

6. Are you able to look to the future with anticipation and joy or are you stuck in the present with no hope of things getting better? _____

7. Have you experienced glory in marital sex in which you feel your mate's spirit flowing into yours?
_____

8. Does your conscience warn you strongly before you do anything, and keep you out of trouble, or does it only work by remorse afterwards? _____

Healing Process

After hearing these questions for the first time at a

retreat setting, a group of six pastors retired to a quiet room where they could discuss among themselves their answers to these questions. First you should be happy to know that none of them answered yes to all the questions. One pastor confessed that he had answered "no" to every question. For the rest of us we each identified particular areas of need in our spiritual life.

The process of healing must always begin with an acknowledgement that there is a problem. Then we must accept responsibility to deal with the problem. It is often easier to continue to blame the people who abused you or hurt you in some other way, but it is not constructive in restoration of a healthy spirit.

Realize that a quick fix will not resolve the issue. There may be quick fixes to improve symptoms, but they will not eliminate the root of the problem. We have to want to be healed badly enough so we are willing to make the effort and face issues we don't want to face. In some ways you can do it yourself, but normally it will require help from others. Admit you need help. Get help! Persist, persist, and persist.

Then you must pray to ask God to help you forgive the one who hurt you. Finally you must pray for God to heal you and fill you with His Spirit.

A child of six thought he was drowning in a swimming pool as an adult playfully held his head under the water. Nobody thought much about the incident, but the child grew up with a constant fear of drowning. Thirty years later, the now young man was seeking a deeper relationship with God. But every time he entered into deep prayer or worship he began to panic. It was the feeling of being immersed in God's Holy Spirit that triggered the panic attack. When we prayed for him he remembered the swimming pool incident and realized that he felt imprisoned in the pool. As he entered into the deeper things of God, it felt like he was back in that pool drowning. He forgave the one who had held him under water, but the panic attacks did not go away. It was several weeks later, while praying to be healed, that he had a vision of being alone in a prison cell. Then Jesus entered the cell and took him by the hand and led him out to freedom. Since then the panic attacks have not returned.

13.   Do you want to be well?

John 5:6 (NKJV) ⁶ When Jesus saw him lying there, and knew that he already had been in that condition a long time, He said to him, "Do you want to be made well?"

Neil was the pastor of a small church back in the mountains east of San Diego. Recently divorced, Neil had a long history of physical, emotional, and spiritual problems. He was seeing professionals for his condition, but Rita and I had been providing prayer, counsel, and emotional support through much of this time. With all this, Neil was not getting any better and in fact it appeared he was falling deeper into depression and failing physically.

On a Friday evening in late fall we were joined by another couple as we drove up to Neil's for another ministry session. His house was in a densely wooded area behind his church. Our meeting went like all other meetings with Neil; a few small breakthroughs, prayers for forgiveness, healing, and deliverance. We sensed no real change until I stopped and asked Neil a question we had never before considered. "Neil, do you want to be healed?"

The question was not asked in desperation or anger, but it was simply put, "Do you really want to be healed?" The question caught us all, including me, by surprise. We could tell that Neil was giving it serious thought. After what seemed like ten minutes, but was probably only one or two, Neil gave us his answer.

"I am not sure that I do want to be well. If I was well, then people would expect more out of me. If I was not sick I would have nothing to hide behind. If I was well, there would be more that I would be required to do."

As a result, Neil decided that it would be better for him to be healed of all his infirmities and return to an effective life and ministry than to continue on the downward spiral. We all agreed that we would help him follow up on his decision.

As we walked out his front door and down the wooden steps I heard something crunch under my foot. The single light bulb above the door gave me enough light to see what I had stepped on. A now dead scorpion had been lying in wait for us as we left the house. Neil's life changed that night for the better. Now remarried and serving a different church his ministry is bearing much fruit.

Luke 10:19 (NKJV) [19] Behold, I give you the authority to trample on serpents and scorpions, and over all the power of the enemy, and nothing shall by any means hurt you.

The question we asked Neil is one to ask ourselves. Do I want to be well?

End notes

[1] Jesus and Addiction, A Prescription to Transform the Dysfunctional Church and Recover Authentic Christianity, 1993 by Recovery Publications

[2] Frank Minerth, et al "Before Burnout: Balanced Living for Busy People" Moody Press, April 1990

[3] Matthew 10:40

[4] Exodus 17:6

[5] Numbers 20:7-11

[6] 1John 2:13-15

[7] Sandford, John, Elijah House Ministries, http://www.elijahhouse.org/

[8] Ezekiel 36:26

[9] Pastor, author of many books and Founder of Elijah House Ministries with his wife Paula

[10] Acts 1:8

[11] Sandford, R. Loren, Wounded Warriors Surviving seasons of stress,Victory House, Tulsa, OK, 1987

[12] Grant Ph.D., Adam M. (2013-04-09). Give and Take: A Revolutionary Approach to Success Penguin Group US.

[13] Sandford, R. Loren, Wounded Warriors Surviving seasons of stress,Victory House, Tulsa, OK, 1987 pp 15

[14] Romans 8:39

[15] John 16:33

[16] Sandford, R. Loren, Wounded Warriors Surviving seasons of stress,Victory House, Tulsa, OK, 1987

[17] Nouwen, Henri, Reaching Out, Image, Reissue Edition, 1986

[18] Lyle E. Schaller, The Interventionist (Abingdon Press; Nashville, 1997)

[19] Romans 12:14-21

[20] Romans 12:19-20

[21] 2Cor5:21 *"God made him who had no sin to be sin for us, so that in him we might become the righteousness of God.*

[22] Acts 5:1-11

[23] Sandford, John L. "Why Some Christians Commit Adultery" Victory House Inc, Tulsa OK (1977)

[24] Sandford, John, "Why Some Christians Commit Adultery" Victory House, Tulsa, 1989

[25] ibid

[26] Revelation 19:10 (NKJV)

[27]   http://www.mayoclinic.org/healthy-living/stress-management/in-depth/exercise-and-stress/art-20044469

[28] http://www.helpguide.org/life/humor_laughter_health.htm

[29] Nouwen, Henri, ",Reaching Out" Image Books, Bantam Doubleday, 1975, NY, NY

[30] (May 1, 1881 – April 10, 1955) French philosopher and Jesuit priest trained as a paleontologist and geologist.

[31] Pascal, Blaise (2012-05-12). Pascal's Pensées (pp. 115-116).   . Kindle Edition.

[32] Sandford, John and Paul, "Healing the Wounded Spirit" Bridge Publishing, South Plainfield, NJ, 1985

[33] Desert Streams Ministries

Author Biography

Bill Johnson is an award-winning author, teacher, and mentor: His writing combines a strong formal education with extensive experience as a leader in ministry and in the scientific community. After many years in the aerospace and naval electronics industries, Bill turned to ministry as a pastor, church planter, and conference speaker.

In 2001 Bill and his wife Rita founded Aslan Ministries, Inc. for the purpose of encouraging and equipping the church and its leaders to become all for which they were created. Bill and Rita have ministered and taught together hundreds of classes throughout the United States, Europe, Asia and the Middle East. Our life scripture is Psalm 71:17-18

Prior to entering full-time ministry, Bill was a successful executive in the electronics industry responsible for starting four profitable entities, and initiated business development throughout the "Pacific Rim."

As a US Army Signal Corps officer, Bill was commanding officer of the first integrated digital data communications networks in the military.

EDUCATION

• Undergraduate studies in Electrical Engineering at Georgia Institute of Technology; and Management and Economics, at University of South Alabama;

• MA Theology, Fuller Theological Seminary.

46832874R10075

Made in the USA
Middletown, DE
02 June 2019